REGARDING MANHATTAN

REGARDING MANHATTAN

John Rosenthal

Sunapee Editions

NEW LONDON · NEW HAMPSHIRE

Sunapee Editions in an imprint of
Safe Harbor Books
P.O. Box 2568
101 Main Street
New London, NH 03257
© 1998

Library of Congress Catalogue Card Number: 98-61120
ISBN: 0-9665798-0-1

This book is dedicated to my parents, Julian and Frances Rosenthal,
who taught me, at just the right age, to love and respect this mysterious city.

Acknowledgements

IN 1967 JEAN MORRISON, poet, novelist, teacher, handed me a Pentax SP500 and a roll of Tri-X film and told me to go outside and look around. He also showed me the photographs of Henri Cartier-Bresson. They were witty and respectful and precise. Looking at them, I understood for the first time that seeing was not, as I supposed, a neutral act, but a very personal one, as self-defining as writing a poem. For this introduction to photography, I thank Jean Morrison.

And thanks, too, to Sy Safransky, who over the years has printed many of my photographs in his magazine, *The Sun*. His editorial conviction that ordinary life, if properly observed, is compelling and luminous has always made good sense to me.

There are many contemporary photographers to whom I am indebted, but none more than Greg Conniff. His counsel on the importance of properly sequencing photographs as a way of defining the shape of their intention has proved invaluable.

I am also grateful to Andy Fleishman who has never doubted the need for enthusiasm; to Alan Shapiro who, on more than one occasion, has led me to my own images; to Wendy Grossman who takes risks others only talk about; to Michael Carty who tells the good, long stories; to Al Ruppersberg who remembers precisely the lost City he has never known; and to Clara Hay who continues to teach me that wisdom and laughter are never strangers.

I have spent many years in New York City, but not always continuously. As a sojourner in the great metropolis, one whose project has been the almost defiantly unprofitable act of strolling about, I have had to rely on the kindness of family and friends. Such kindness cannot be repaid, but it must be acknowledged. A thank you then to my aunt and uncle, Kate and Herbert Rosenthal, who offered their hospitality—without reserve or stipulation—whenever the need arose. And equal thanks to Ken Horowitz, the man who owns this town, a cynical, joyous, pugnacious, sweet-hearted wiseguy, my friend and companion all these years. Thanks, Kenny, for putting me up all those years ago in that East Village. And, yes, thanks for saving my neck at Coney Island. I can still see you running down the boardwalk, shouting, "Is there a problem here?" just as that guy was about to dismantle my camera and the photographer who owned it.

Finally, I'd like to thank my wife, Paula Press, and my two children, Laura and John Keats. Love is, I think, the best safeguard against the befuddlements of cynicism. If I have managed to remain surprised and even delighted by this mysterious city year after year, it is mostly to you that I owe the favor.

Introduction

WHAT I REMEMBER MOST VIVIDLY about my first visit to New York City in the early summer of 1968 was looking up at the sky as I walked from the Trailways Bus Terminal over to Fifth Avenue. I had come from Boston to see my brother, who had a small role in an off-Broadway musical. I grew up in the vicinity of Boston and saw myself as a city kid. So I felt ready enough for the densely crowded streets, the shrill knots of traffic, and even the half-exhilarating, half-terrifying sense of freedom I felt in my total anonymity, the simultaneous feeling that I could do anything here where no one knew me and that nothing I did would matter to anyone. I felt, as I often did wandering in downtown Boston, or through Harvard Square, utterly liberated and utterly inconsequential.

Nothing in my previous experience, though, prepared me either for the colossal scale of buildings looking over buildings, buildings so tall and massive that they seemed less to rise upward from the ground than to descend earthward from the sky, bearing an overwhelming human gravity, or the way those towering yet oddly makeshift, improvised, uneven structures (on the side streets especially) blocked out so much of the overcast sky, squeezing it into fragmented chevrons, jagged triangles, patches and strips of gray light that squinted down through the narrow openings between the blocks, and along the avenues. Even the sky there bore the gigantic imprint of human desire, human work.

All that day I walked. I kept on walking. There was something in the city itself that wouldn't let me stop: in the flashes of midtown sky; in the grand display windows in which my own and every other passer-by's reflections seemed to swim blurringly across the flawless surfaces of so many things I couldn't dream of buying; in the snatches of languages, the bit and pieces of conversation I overheard at the corners where people jostled or brushed as they massed together, waiting for the light to change; in the abrasive rhythms of people going into and out of doorways, in and out of taxis, dawdling or hurrying, all carried along within the separate yet interweaving channels of their desires—indeed, the city seemed like a fever dream extension of the inchoate adolescent longing for excitement, for women, for longing itself, that kept me walking all the way down Fifth Avenue to Washington Square, and back uptown again. Everything was at one and the same time too much and not enough, elusive and all pervasive, immediate and out of reach.

The photographs in John Rosenthal's *Regarding Manhattan* instruct us on how to find the still points of the moving city, those evanescent junctures of experience when the contradictory and competing ideas enacted by the city define and clarify each other. His photographs of crowded streets are spacious with loneliness as well as possibility, just as his solitary views of squares or parks insinuate both the persistence and displacement of a kind of pastoral dream within the urban world.

One of the book's principal obsessions is the tension between energy and structure, the natural and the artificial, anarchic spirit and repressive form. His enclosed, blurred, nearly spectral view of expressionless commuters seen through a dirty subway window is made more ghostly and insubstantial by the stark, though battered metallic clarity of the train's exterior, the stenciled numbers, 696, to the left of the window, and the reflection of the bright incandescent segments of fluorescent station lighting in the upper pane of glass. The contrasts between light and dark, sharp metal and vaporous flesh, the ghostly human forms and the preternatural vividness of the machine that holds them, all dramatize the fragility of personal identity (or the hope of any I-and-Thou relation) within the everyday, impersonal, cramped spaces of urban life.

Rosenthal's most sardonic treatment of the uneasy relation between form and instinct is his underground view of the polar bear tank in the Central Park Zoo. The polar bear has just plunged into the water, and the blurred shape of its great bulk, and the volumes of bright and shadowy water it has displaced, form a powerful image of natural energy hemmed in by brick and glass, put on display behind a wire fence, right there before us yet entirely withheld. Our culturally mediated connection to the animal world itself and to the animal life within us, to internal and external nature, is suggested by the still wet and open umbrella lying on its side to the right of the tank. Whereas the polar bear is immersed in water, his natural element, we sport umbrellas to keep ourselves from getting wet.

Rosenthal treats the same theme in a more lyrical but no less ironic light in a studiously composed yet resonant photograph of a frozen pond, white with snow, in Central Park along 59th Street. The gigantic wall of apartment buildings dominates the background of the picture. A strip of sunlight that has slipped through a gap in the buildings brightens a thin band of snow where a human figure is caught in mid-leap, arms and legs outstretched, back arched. The image is one of unrestrained exuberance, but an exuberance that is qualified not only by the massive weight of buildings in the background, but also by the shadow that the upflung body casts against the thin band of sunlight that contains it. The shadow, staining the bright snow with the gray tonality of the shadowed pond, seems to remind the viewer of all the cultural gravity that the leaping figure has momentarily escaped.

In this photograph, and in the others of the city in winter, what snow or fog enable Rosenthal to do is to simplify his view, eliminate extraneous detail, in order to perceive the city in the city, or the structural idea or dream of city life obscured within the agitated clutter of the every day. In another Central Park photograph, we look down a vast, deserted, tree-lined vista on a late December day. The calligraphic wickerwork of branches curling over the rain-slick tarmac grows paler and paler as the view recedes until the trees dissolve entirely into a ball of radiant fog. What the fog obscures, of course, is the city itself, the city as it now is, with all its mess and strife, its continuous levellings and renewals, yet what replaces it is not the city as it once was, but the city that the park imagines, or its planners did, the city as a human settlement that still provides within its very heart a solitary pastoral retreat from city life. It is as if the city were a kind of palimpsest that the snow or fog erases just enough for the photographer to read within the context of the present moment the older writing of another era's dreams and aspirations. That such dreams and aspirations have only momentary purchase on the present, that the vision itself is evanescent, contingent on the accidents of weather, is suggested by the way the trees reflected in the tarmac's wrinkling, rain-wet sheen swirl indecipherably away like ink in water.

In the book's most somber and brooding snowscape, we look across an empty Broadway at the Empire and Liberty Theatres. It is late at night, and the only signs of traffic are the horizontal ridges left in the snow along the street. The blank marquees seem to steam with light as they protrude out over the sidewalk, bearing their radiant names and dwarfing the few pedestrians who trudge home through the thick snow, each of them bent over, it seems, as much from the heavy weight of all that shining, as from the shopping bags they carry and the snow they push through. The words "Empire" and "Liberty" are fraught with political and social history. They represent the grand official promises of the American experiment, the sloganeering ideals of plentitude, opportunity, and freedom. That these old theatres had become by the 1980's two of the seedier ones on Times Square, have now been closed down, and will soon make way for a Disney "Family Entertainment" complex, invests the image with a poignant irony. Rosenthal pictures the theatres and, by extension the city itself, at a moment of transition, when the heterogenous, abrasive and seamy culture of Times Square is being sanitized and made hospitable for more affluent consumers. The captured moment is fine, for here in the blank but ostentatious marquees, pulsing with empty radiance, is nothing less than a proclamation of lost memory.

If the photographs mourn the passing of an older, denser, more humanly complicated New York, and worry over the emergence of a safer, corporate-driven, more homogenous but no less acquisitive urban landscape, they nonetheless preserve and, by preserving, also sustain the very values imperilled by the city's renovations. Every song of lament is simultaneously a song of praise; we only mourn the passing of the things we cherish. And what the images in *Regarding Manhattan* teach us how to cherish is the overwhelming, sometimes dangerous, yet always enlivening disorder and multiplicity of pleasure, ambition, and desire embodied in this most American of cities.

ALAN SHAPIRO

". . . always unprepared, even years later with a camera in my hands for the mid-morning sun slicing down Mott Street and bouncing off the dead eyes of sea bass cooling in a tub of ice; for the midnight snow falling on West End Avenue where once, in a blizzard, I watched Miles Davis dance a rumba in a long mink coat; for the tall, smiling man in the pork pie hat and the elegant, slightly stained suit, who stood in front of the Plaza Hotel and nodded gently at all who passed, saying "It's all over"; for the warranted glory of buildings that are simply beautiful; for the dog man on 77th who jumped off a bench in the middle of Broadway, barking, and scared me witless; for the word-of-mouth that keeps artists — exiled from small towns in North Carolina and Ohio — alive; for the Sunday Central Park festivals of bared flesh and sweet motion and Pakistani rock and roll; for the hint of danger on small paths and the flicking eyes of lonely men; for the nightime city seen high on rooftops, its avenues blinking like pin-ball machines with red and green and yellow and occasionally blue lights; and above all, unprepared for the sheer civility of it all, the vast human contrivance that permits millions to pass each other and not to bump, and to live high in the sky and not to fall."

JOHN ROSENTHAL, "Remembering The City"

REGARDING MANHATTAN

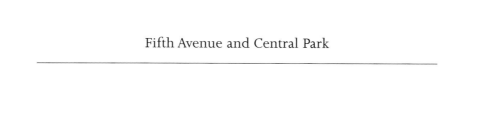

Fifth Avenue and Central Park

9th Street and Avenue A

Tompkins Square Park—Early Morning

Fifth Avenue and 42nd Street

John Keats Rosenthal at Yankee Stadium

Third Avenue

Tompkins Square—Albino Boxer

Spring Street

Christopher Street

Central Park

Central Park — Unmoored Boat

Tompkins Square Park—Early Morning

Coney Island

Coney Island

1st Avenue

Tommy Thompson at the Whitney Museum

Central Park—Beginning of Snow Storm

Jump Seats in Checker Cab

Third Avenue

Subway Window

Mulberry Street—Italian Seamen's Club

Mulberry Street

Central Park—Janet's Song

Coney Island

Central Park Zoo—Polar Bear and Umbrella

Museum of Natural History

West Side Pier

Park Avenue

_____

Central Park

Times Square Subway Station

Times Square—Blizzard of 1996

East 8th Street—Photographer and Model

East 10th Street and Avenue C—Jean Morrison, Poet

East 9th Street

Lexington Avenue—Bloomingdale's in Snow

42nd Street — The Liberty and Empire Theatres

42nd Street

Central Park and 59th Street—Frozen Pond

Times Square

Central Park—The Ramble

Regarding Manhattan
was printed in an edition of 1,000 copies at
The Stinehour Press, Lunenburg Vermont.
The photographs were reproduced as 300-line-screen
duotones on Warren Lustro Dull text.
Bound at Acme Bookbinding, Charlestown, MA
Designed by Dean Bornstein

DATE DUE

MAR 3 1999	
OCT 13 2000	
MAY 1 2003	
OCT 27 2004	